TABLE OF CONTENTS

A WORD ABOUT GRAMMER AND SPELLING

There are mistakes in this book, I guarantee it.

Where are the mistakes? Heck if I know. If I did, I would fix them. But since I don't, they remain.

Don't get me wrong, I'm all for trying to spell things correctly and using grammar that hopefully makes my words easier to read.

However, I'm not willing to let perfect grammar and spelling hold up the works. I want to get this information out to you. I could spend a lot of time and money having editors go over and over this text to make sure it's absolutely perfect, but I think it's more important that I get this information in your hands – even if it has some mistakes.

Mark Twain once said, "I don't give a damn for a man that can only spell a word one way."

Since I want you to give a damn about getting a great internship, please forgive me if I spell a word more than one way here.

1 THE SYSTEM IS RIGGED

That's right, it's rigged.

School, for the most part, is based on fairness. Teachers (in theory, at least) are supposed to grade tests and papers objectively. Students generally have equal access to information. If somebody has a special needs, schools and teachers do what they can to level the field.

The working world and getting an internship is not a fair process. If you expect that it is, you will be disappointed. If you dwell on the notion that finding an internship should be fair, let me humbly suggest that you are wasting your time and missing the point.

Has the process for getting an internship ever been fair? I don't think so. One need only look back through history to realize that apprentices, squires, ladies in waiting, aide de camps – pretty much every version of what we would now call an internship have never been a completely equal employment opportunity.

Labor laws (and let's hope in most cases just basic human decency) require that employers not discriminate in their hiring practices based on things like gender, race, sexual orientation, religion, etc.. However, there are plenty of other things they can use discriminate one internship applicant from another.

Thank goodness there are. If you think about it, employers NEED something to discriminate one internship applicant from another. Suppose you are reviewing a stack of internship applications.

Going through the stack, you would likely be on the lookout for any clues that can help you decide whether the application in hand should go in the "yes" pile or the "no" pile. You might even find yourself shouting out loud, begging for any applicant to give you a reason to put you in the "yes" pile. You could find yourself saying something along the lines of "APPLICANTS! For the LOVE OF PEAT! HELP ME HELP YOU!"

How do I know that your internship application might get yelled at? I know because over the years I've yelled at plenty and know colleagues who have yelled at their fair share of internship applications.

Time after time I see would-be interns making the same basic mistakes with how they go about trying to get an internship. **It's almost as if we took**

all young people and put them in room and gave them bad information about how the working world works.

Wait. Oh shit. That's exactly what we've done.

The working world is SO DIFFERENT from school. Until you experience this difference firsthand you may not realize how great the difference is, much less believe it. I see it all the time: students who do amazingly well in school have a really hard time finding their way in the workplace because they've never been taught about the differences between work, and school.

Some schools have caught onto this and offer classes about internships and the working world, but not many.

Techniques you used as a student that led to success: getting into certain colleges, landing a part in the play, or making a spot on the team probably won't work very well during your internship hunt. Why? They won't work because the system is rigged.

The things you think will help you get an internship probably won't; assume the process will not be fair.

If that weren't enough, the internship world is reaching new levels of competitiveness. Twenty or even ten years ago, internships weren't such the big deal that they are today.

The National Association of Colleges and Employers (NACE) estimates that intern hiring will increase by 8.5% in the next year, and it shows no sign of slowing down. As information about internships becomes more accessible, as students are pressured to get extra credentials under their belt in a fierce job market, the search for great internships will continue to be more and more competitive.

So what the heck does this mean for you?

It means that the stakes are higher than ever before. Having one or more internships under your young professional belt is no longer optional. But, if you can land that perfect internship and use it to access special information and people, then you potential benefits are huge.

Realize right now that, if you're going to be competitive in the working world, you can't play fair.

Now, don't get me wrong, I'm not talking about cheating or stealing your co-workers' lunch money, or being a bully, or being somehow malicious.

But I am saying that you should forget about playing by the rules you've been taught. If you want to get a great internship, you should drop a lot of the assumptions you have about what will make an employer want to mentor you as an intern.

In order to land that perfect internship, you need to give yourself an unfair advantage.

Those who get this unfair advantage will stand out like a blinking bright light to potential employers. Those who have this unfair advantage will make reviewers of internship applications stop, sit bank, take a drink of Diet Coke, and say, "Dear Lord, finally, at long last, thank you for putting this application in my hands." Those who have this unfair advantage will have an adamantium edge when it comes to getting a great internship.

When I started out in my career I would have given a lot to get the edge that the information in this book is going to give you. During the early days of my career I was pretty clueless.

My family moved to Thailand when I was just a kid and I wound up spending most of my formative years there. I attended the International School of Bangkok with kids from all over. It was completely awesome and most of my best friends in the world are ones I made there.

Growing up as an expatriate kid in Thailand was an incredible learning experience and gave me a lot of skills, but successfully navigating the modern career world was not one of them.

I came to the U.S. to attend college but in the span of 4 years I managed to transfer schools SEVEN times.

Why did I transfer so many times? Well…to say I was "searching" is an understatement. I had no framework for thinking about a future career, and I really didn't understand the dynamics of the working world at all. Instead of staying in any one place long enough to have a chance to figure it out, I just kept moving.

By the time I had done enough to earn my undergraduate degree, I was working as a scuba instructor on Guam. I spent 3 or 4 hours a day under the ocean with the fish and the octopuses and the puffer fish. It was excellent. I didn't have to worry about wearing shoes or taking tests or my future career at all. I didn't have to worry about anything other than keeping my students safe and communing with the fish.

Several years out of school, underwater with the fish, in one of the most remote places on earth – I had never even heard the word "internship" much less understand what an "internship" was.

Maybe I was the sunburned, maybe it was the salt, maybe it was sand – but after three years in the ocean, I started getting restless again. I felt like my brain was getting spongy; it needed to be used. So, I started to think about the possibility of going to graduate school.

Was my interest in grad school based on a clear career strategy? Hell no. I was looking for my next refuge. I still had no idea about a clear career path; I requested applications from schools and programs of all sorts.

By the way, this was all pre-Internet and I was on a tiny island in the middle of the Pacific Ocean. So, applying to schools involved taking out an actual piece of a paper and writing, "Dear University X, Please send me information about your graduate program in Ancient Babylonian Cabinet Making."

Slowly but surely, applications and information started arrive in my mailbox. Perhaps because I had transferred so many times as an undergrad I was a whiz at filling out applications and I sent out a ton. I applied to law schools, engineering schools, public policy programs, a couple of seminaries – the shot gun approach. My grad school application strategy was very much based on throwing out a bunch of stuff to see what stuck.

After sending out about 15 applications, I was on a roll and just a teensy bit inspired. I thought to myself, "I'm scuba instructor on Guam – that's pretty cool. But what would be a cooler job than that?" My answer: The White House.

So, I sent off another one of my letters to 1600 Pennsylvania Avenue. It was something along the lines of, "Dear President Clinton, How can I come and work for you?" I dropped it off at the Guam post office and figured I would never hear back a thing.

However, to my great surprise, several weeks later I received a response in a very official looking White House envelope. It was a White House internship application.

I had never heard of an "internship" but, it sounded pretty good to me. So, I put my superior application writing skills to work and sent that puppy off. Again, I figured I would never hear back. But, I managed to get the cool

White House envelope (which I kept) so I figured that was a pretty good deal.

Fast forward about five months later: I was accepted into the graduate program in International Affairs at George Washington University in Washington, DC. So, with a single backpack, sun bleached hair, and flip flops, I headed off to the nation's capitol.

As an ocean transplant, setting myself up to live and work in Washington, DC is a story unto itself. But I managed to do it. One morning, after the dust had settled from my arrival, I went for a run around the National Mall. As I passed the White House I thought, "Man, those bastards never even sent me a rejection letter for that internship thing. I should call them." So, I did.

I responded to the lady on the phone by saying "YES!" and "Thank you!" After saying goodbye my first thought was, "I need a suit."

How did I manage to get a great internship? I got lucky. In hindsight I now realize that during my quest for a great internship I actually did a lot of things right without even realizing it.

I'm so glad to be able to provide the information in this book to you because it means you don't need to rely on luck, you can go after a great internship the right way. **You can get a great internship by getting an unfair advantage.**

How do you get an unfair advantage in your search for a great internship? Keep reading, comrade.

2 GETTING AN UNFAIR ADVANTAGE

If you want to get a great internship, you need to get an unfair advantage. Does the word "unfair" make you uncomfortable? Get over it.

If you are in school, or if you've just left school, I can understand why the notion of being "unfair" might make you nervous. School is a fair place. But remember, **the working world is not a fair place**.

That is why you need an unfair advantage. Having this unfair advantage will show potential employers that you are mature beyond the years of your professional experience. Having this unfair advantage will make you stand out from the crowd.

Will you ever use the unfair advantage to manipulate or hurt colleagues? If you want to go very far in your career you won't.

The unfair advantage I'm talking about only works if it comes from a place of authenticity. In the long term, the unfair advantage I'm going to teach you in this book will only work for positive, constructive purposes.

Warning: if you attempt to use the unfair advantage to get an internship for malicious purposes, it won't work.

On the other hand, if you want to quickly and pretty easily establish an unfair advantage so you can get a great internship for the right reasons…well, you've come to the right place.

99% of students applying to internships today will go about getting an internship kind of haphazardly, without a plan. The internships a lot of these students wind up doing will likely reflect this lackluster strategy.

However, by understanding the four steps you must take to establish an unfair advantage when seeking an internship, you can get a great one. To establish an unfair advantage and get great internship you must:

Choose a Great Internship

Find a Great Internship

Apply for a Great Internship

Land a Great Internship

Before I dive into each of these, let me give you a sneak peek into each…

<u>Step One: Choose a Great Internship</u>

This is the step most young professionals always forget. Before you can get a great internship, you must understand why you want an internship! Just because you can get an internship doesn't mean it is the internship you should choose.

Step Two: Find a Great Internship

Once you know why you want to do an internship and have an idea about what kind of internship would be great for you, you've got to find it! Internships don't just grow on trees, you know. Well, maybe some of the agricultural ones do, but I digress.

Step Three: Apply for a Great Internship

After you find a great internship, you must apply to it. This is really the nuts and bolts of getting a great internship. Applying for a great internship is more art than science, and you definitely don't want to play fair here.

Step Four: Land a Great Internship

You know why you want to do an internship, you've found the right internship and you've sent them an application – this is where you close the deal.

Four steps, that's all there is to it. Think there is no way you can get a great internship? Are you intimidated by the process of looking for an internship? Don't be.

If you put in just a little bit of thought, a little bit of effort, and follow these four steps, you can get a great internship. Let me tell you more.

PART I: YOU CHOOSE

Why do you want to do an internship? Do you know?

If you want to make friends, go to a party or join a social club. If you want an excuse to live in new exciting place for the summer, you don't need an internship to do it, just go. If you want to do an internship just because you think it'll make you look good, don't bother; your future potential employers will be able to tell when an internship is just a window dressing on your resume. If you want to do an internship because you're in love and girl and/or boy of dreams is there, don't do it…stalker.

In my book, "<u>Your Last Day of School: 56 Ways to Be a Great Intern and Turn Your Internship into a Job</u>" I argue that there are really only two good reasons to do an internship. They are:

To get access to special information

To get access to special people

Internships are a guided learning experience – they involve special person (a mentor) who offers special information (stuff you want to learn). That's it. If your goal in pursuing an internship is anything else, there are better uses of your time.

That being said however, those two reasons cover a lot of situations – maybe even yours. When choosing an internship, here are some things to think about.

3 YOU KNOW

Maybe you just know what internship you want to do. You know what you want to do with your life and you know what kind of internship will let you rub shoulders with experts in a specific field and let you learn specialized information.

Is that you? If so, congratulations! Your path forward is pretty clear. Suppose you want to dedicate your life to the study of Himalayan tectonics. I haven't looked it up, but I'll bet money there are just a few organizations in the world who study that. Go find an internship with one of them.

On the other hand, if this isn't you – is there any chance it could be?

In other words, what if you did some thinking that would let you eliminate your options? This goes against a lot of advice you might have received in the past about the importance of being "well-rounded" and a "Renaissance" person.

The word "decision" comes from the Latin root "caedere," which means "to cut." It might be worth your while to do some deciding. Cut away some options. **If you cut away enough, you might just find the answer to the question "what do I want to do?"**

One of Sherlock Holmes' favorite sayings is, "eliminate all other factors, and the one which remains must be the truth." Start cutting.

There's one other way you can get a clue about "what you want to do." Go over all your options, and then ask yourself, "Which of these excites me?" If there is one that jumps out at you – it's a good bet that you should go do that.

When considering your life's professional purpose, realize that the more specific you can get, the better you will be. Find a real niche. Don't decide you want to do work related to women's literacy. Rather, decide you are going to be the world's expert on women's English literacy relating to the northeastern part of Botswana on a Tuesday with regard to girls between the ages of 8 and 12 who were orange on Tuesday's when it rains. Get specific and go deep, not wide.

Also, **realize that whatever you choose to do in the world to make money doesn't necessarily mean you have to give up your other passions.** In fact, you may want to avoid doing the things you really love for money altogether or run the risk of turning something you love into a "job."

The point I want to make is that, if you can, decide on the thing you want to make your profession. Narrow it down. Then, decide you're going to do an internship in that.

4 YOU NEED TO EXPLORE

Do you want to use an internship to explore your career options?

Stop.

Go back and read the chapter just before this one. Is there any way you can narrow your options before attempting to choose an internship? Have you interviewed some people in the fields that are your top contenders? Have you spoken to a good career counselor about the competing options?

If so and you're truly at an impasse, know that using an internship as a way to get exposure to a new career is legit – but it's not as good an option as going into an internship knowing what you want to do.

Have I made you feel guilty enough about not knowing what you want to do with the rest of your life? Sorry. It's just that I don't want you to waste time if you don't need to.

Let me let you in on a little secret. It is very rare that one is completely convinced they are fulfilling their life's purpose professionally. Some people can say they are completely sure, but it's rare. **When you're 30, you're probably still going to wonder. When you're 40, you'll likely still wonder. When you're 50 you'll still wonder.** It may sound crazy, but if you have a list of options that all seem possible – consider flipping a coin.

In her essay "Wear Sunscreen," (popularized in song by Baz Luhrmann) Mary Schmich writes,

"Don't feel guilty if you don't know what you want to do with your life. The most interesting people I know didn't know at 22 what they wanted to do with their lives; some of the most interesting 40 year olds I know still don't….Your choices are half chance, so are everybody else's."

If you must, it's ok to use an internship to explore a possible career. Just don't mess around too long – make narrowing down your options a constant goal. The sooner you do, the faster and closer you'll get to finding a professional purpose that is truly fulfilling. Perhaps even more importantly, the faster you discover a fulfilling professional course, the faster you will master it, become the world's expert at it, and become incredibly in demand for it.

5 THE LONG INTERVIEW

If and when you are clear about your professional future, you may be looking to do an internship with an organization because you want to find a job there.

Is this a good reason to do an internship? You bet your sweet bippy it is.

Let me ask you a question. If you are somebody responsible for hiring others, are you going to hire somebody who has already been interning for you, who already knows the work, and who has been doing a tremendous job? Or, are you going to hire somebody who is a relative unknown quantity?

Do the math.

One way to think of an internship is to think of it as an "extended job interview."

Now, some don't think that's fair. They say it's exploitative to keep a student young professional on hold until a job opens up. They're right, it's not fair. If you dwell on fairness, you won't get very fair when it comes to internships. That's why you want an unfair advantage.

Is the concept of an "extended job interview" exploitative? Assuming we're not talking about a forced labor situation, or something that involves coercion or threats – I don't think it is exploitative. If you're doing an internship and you feel you're being exploited, leave immediately.

However, if you're interning at a place where expectations are clear and you've been given an honest appraisal about the likelihood of your being hired, where you still feel it's in your interest to stay - then you should stick. Stick around and be such a great intern that they'll bend over backwards to hire you.

6 DRESS REHEARSAL

"I need experience to find a job, but I need a job to gain experience!"

Does this paradox sound familiar to you? If so, you're not along. The whole work/experience trap is a catch-22 that a lot of young professionals run into. Is an internship a good way to escape this chicken and the egg trap? Yes.

Maybe you don't know what you want to do with the rest of your life, but you just need some grown-up credentials. You want some experience, any experience, that will give your resume a little gravitas. An internship may be the answer.

Don't get me wrong, if you know that you want to spend the rest of your life studying Bahamanian underwater basket weaving, then you better be on the next plane to Nassau.

However if that's not you and you just want some experience under your belt, then go ahead. Take an internship that is going to expose you to the generic working world.

There are some skills that apply to pretty much any working environment and, if the working world is new to you, you can learn these skills pretty much anywhere. For example, if you've never sat through a business meeting – they're pretty much the same wherever you go. There may be some nuances, but a business meeting is pretty much the same creature wherever you go.

In addition, generic experience gained through an internship can teach you a lot about skills you'll need outside the office. If you're interested in getting exposure to all the stuff professionals do outside the office (figuring out dry cleaning, getting to work on time, building professional discipline), then you can benefit from pretty much any internship.

Is the search for generic working experience the best reason to choose an internship? No. Is it still a legit reason for some? You bet.

7 THE MOUNTAIN

When George Mallory was asked why he wanted to climb Mount Everest, he famously replied, "Because it's there."

You may choose to do an internship for the same reason…because it's there.

In my experience the Universe has a way of putting opportunities in front of people for a reason. It's not always true, but a lot of times I believe it is.

So, if you suddenly find yourself with nothing to do for the summer but your uncle's friend's brother's cousin has an internship opening at her Irish-Mexican fusion test kitchen…well, Erin Go Bragh amigo!

Again, I want you to be strategic with the internship you choose. But, if an internship comes out of the blue and it seems interesting, and you've got nothing else going on…take that internship.

For young professionals living in or near big cities, the internship choices may abound. But if you live somewhere where internship options limited and if practical considerations require that you stay put, then convenience may drive your internship choice.

Of course, the limitations of space and time are becoming less and less of a factor with the dramatic increase in the availability of virtual internships. More and more students and employers are taking advantage of technology engage in internships online.

Through a virtual internship, a student in rural Nebraska can do internship work for a graphic design company in London without having to travel to the UK, worry about visas, finding a place to live, or really even worry about the time difference.

I think practical considerations are a fine reason to pick an internship. But if your internship options are limited and you don't want to be practical, be virtual.

8 THE ALMIGHTY DOLLAR

In a perfect world, education would be free.

In a perfect world there would be no such thing as tuition and teachers would be among the highest paid professionals in our society. Of course, we do not live in a perfect world.

Nonetheless, some forms of education come pretty close to free. In the U.S. tax payer-funded public schools offer education to everyone at no charge. We have a range of student loan and scholarship programs available to help make college a real possibility for almost anyone who wants to go.

But I think the purest form of free education are internships where an employer says, "come work here and we'll teach you." Sure, a student must devote time and energy – but that's true with any form of education.

Internships aren't about getting paid.

However, some people get hung up on the pay thing. They believe that in order for an internship to have value, an intern must be paid.

It's a debate that could fill a whole book, so I'm not going to get into here other than to say: if you're trying to get an internship because you want to earn money, you shouldn't be trying to get an internship, you should be trying to get a job.

Is there anything wrong with internships that pay? Of course not! If you find an internship that pays, more power to you.

What I'm saying here however is that you shouldn't let the question of pay factor into what internship you're trying to get.

You may be in a tough financial situation. You may be in a situation where you can't afford to do an internship full-time. If that's you I sympathize – I've been there.

So, treat the situation just as you would if you needed to be a part-time student. Go find the highest paying job you can doing whatever part-time so you can afford to do an internship with the rest of your time.

If you're a young professional and you want to get an internship, this is not the time to faint of heart. Cut every bit of extra fat out of your living expenses. Live lean.

Living lean means living for free with friends or relatives when you can, it means public transportation, it means living off peanut butter and jelly for a lot of the week. It means no video games or shopping for fancy shoes; no frills.

Think that is too tough? Are you unwilling to take such drastic measures? If not, rest assured, your competition will. **How far are you willing to go to overcome financial challenges in order to get a great internship? It's your choice.**

When I did my first internship I woke up at 3:15 am daily so I could report to a job from 4 am to 10 am so I could do my internship from 10 am to 6 pm, and then attend classes from 6 pm to 9 pm.

Was I tired? I was totally tired. Was it worth it in the end? It was absolutely worth it and I would do it again. If I did it, you can too.

Don't let money stand in the way of your education any more than you must. Don't let financial challenges effect what internship you choose any more than you must.

9 TAKE REFUGE

There is one more really good reason to do an internship that a lot of people overlook. That reason is: you need to take refuge.

Statistics reflecting unemployment or underemployment among students coming out of college are off the chart. If you've made it through the gauntlet of higher education and are now crossing what seems to be a desert of unemployment, getting an internship might be the oasis you need.

It is often said that finding a job is much easier when you have a job. I think this is absolutely true. But of course, when you don't have a job, that's a real catch-22, isn't it?

If you think getting an internship that will force you to get out of a rut, to wake up at a certain time in the morning and actually go to the trouble of bathing, you might be right. If you think going to an internship and just doing something productive with your day might give you the energy you need to traverse the unemployment dessert you're currently trying to cross, I think you might be onto something.

Because you're reading this book and you've actually made it this far, I suspect you are a person that has some kind of work ethic. I believe you are the sort of person who takes pride in doing things that are useful with your time.

When one goes from having a crazy class schedule to exams to nothing, and all of their social networks from college have dispersed, well…that can be shocking. This transition can knock the tar out of pretty much anybody.

If you need a refuge where you can regroup, an internship might give you the structure you need.

10 ALL-ACCESS PASS

Some who are critical of internships claim that only the blue-blooded and privileged can ever get them. I think this is dead wrong.

Do some students and young professionals get internships because of family and/or political connections? Yep. Is that how things generally work in the working world? Sometimes. Is that fair? Nope.

This is why you need an unfair advantage.

Let's suppose you come have some kind of disadvantaged or unusual background – as in, you don't summer in the Hamptons at the country club with Todd and Margie. If you apply to an internship and somebody rejects you because of your ethnicity, sexual orientation, religion, age, economic status, or whatever – let me be clear, they suck.

First, they're most likely breaking some pretty major laws. But, more important than that – they're probably not somebody you will learn very much from during an internship.

In my experience, most internships aren't like that. In fact, I've seen plenty of cases where employers use internship programs to help diversify their workplace both in the internship program itself and for interns that kick butt, as a recruitment tool for staff positions.

In this way, an internship can provide an avenue for people to access organizations, no matter who they are.

If you feel like you're being held back because of where you come from or who you are, doing an internship might unlock more doors than you imagine.

PART II: I KNOW YOU'RE OUT THERE SOMEWHERE

At this point you may be asking yourself, "how can I choose an internship before I find one?"

I want you to understand: don't choose an internship from the ones you find. Instead, find an internship based on the one you choose.

Once you've made a choice about the sort of internship you want to do, and you know why you've made that choice, only then you will be prepared to find the right internship for you.

In many ways choosing an internship is a more difficult process than finding an internship. Once you limit your choices, narrow your search area, and know what you're looking for, finding a great internship becomes much easier.

11 INTERNSHIP SITES

In today's day and age, the obvious place to look for internships is…online.

But often the easiest places to look aren't always the best places to look. Especially if you're hoping to avoid competition against the bazillions of other students trying to find an internship the exact same way, you might want to consider trying to find an internship via alternative routes.

However, there are a ton of online resources to help students find internships. There are plenty of places worth a look; here are some of the main ones.

Disclaimer: not all internship sites are created equal. As with anything online, you should use your good judgment when giving out personal information or paying somebody money to help you get an internship.

That being said, I think these sites are some of the best places to start an internship search:

<u>The Big Free Ones</u>

Indeed (http://indeed.com)

In my opinion this is the grand poobah of internship and job and internship searching sites. It aggregates listings from a ton of places. A great place to start. It's free.

Craigslist (http://craigslist.com)

This is perhaps the MOST overlooked place to find great internships, especially local internships and internships with small organizations. If you want to find internships that a lot of people don't know about, this is the place online.

Internships.com (http://internships.com)

This is another heavy hitter in the internship world. Lots of internships to be found here. It's free, though they also offer a premium service that you pay for.

USAJobs (http://usajobs.gov)

If you're looking to find an internship for the federal government, this is the place to look. It's a massive directory, but often lists internships right along with other federal job opportunities.

Also Really Good Free General Sites

Ideallist (http://ideallist.org)

Experience.com (http://experience.com)

Simplyhired (http://simplyhired.com)

These three are all big job listing aggregators, but they often list a bunch of internships; they are similar to Indeed

Great Free Sites That Focus On Just Internships

Youtern (http://youtern.com)

Full disclosure, I work closely with these guys and I think they are awesome. Their site lists plenty of unique internship opportunities you might not find anyplace else, especially with small start-up companies.

Intern Match (http://internmatch.com)

Great service that focuses on listing just internship opportunities.

Super Interns (http://superinterns.com)

The folks at super interns don't have listings on their site, but they know about a lot of internship opportunities. Definitely worth taking a look. Also, the two ladies that run super interns are SUPER nice.

The Intern Queen (http://internqueen.com)

Lauren Berger has a huge following – and she lists lots of internships that you may not see elsewhere. Definitely worth checking out.

Some Pay Sites

Intern Qube (http://internqube.com)

This site has a minimal subscription fee and was created by Michael True, one of the most respected internship experts in the nation.

The Internship Series (http://www.internships-usa.com)

Check to see if your school subscribes to this service, if it does, the Internship Series online lists a bunch of opportunities.

Dream Careers (http://summerinternships.com)

This site encourages students to apply and then offers internship placement for a hefty fee. Dream Careers' business model has received criticism, but some students are happy with the service, so I list it here.

<u>Internships In Washington, DC</u>

Capitol Hill

(http:/www. senate.gov/employment/po/positions.htm)

(http://www.house.gov/content/jobs)

The House and Senate employ a ton of interns, you can find out about some of these opportunities through their respective employment bulletins.

Brad Traverse (http://bradtraverse.com)

This former Hill Staffer charges a small monthly fee to see his daily DC job and internship listings.

Tom Manatos (http://tommanatos.com)

This former Hill guy does the same.

DC Public Affairs & Communications Jobs Blog

(http://publicaffairsjobs.blogspot.com)

Gordon Barnes' runs an awesome blog that has plenty of DC internship listings. It's free.

The Washington Center (http://twc.edu)

This nonprofit places students in internships for a tuition fee. It's been around forever and has placed thousands upon thousands of students over the years.

Other nonprofits that charge tuition fees to place students with internships in Washington, DC are:

The Washington Internship Institute (http://www.wiidc.org)

The Fund for American Studies (http://dcinternships.org)

<u>Internships In New York, NY</u>

New York Creative Interns (http://nycreativeinterns.com)

If you're looking for an internship in NYC, especially in advertising and/or the creative sector, this site is worth a visit.

<u>Internships Outside the USA</u>

Intern Abroad (http://internabroad.com)

Part of a larger study abroad site, this web page offers listings about internship opportunities overseas.

Inspiring Interns (http://inspiringinterns.com)

If you're looking for an internship in the UK, look for inspiration here.

Internshala (http://internshala.com)

If you're looking for an internship in India, Sarvesh is the guy to talk to.

Of course in addition to all these sites, individual organizations often list information about internship programs on their own websites. Don't forget to look there too.

Do you know about another great internship site that I missed? If so, let me know!

12 UNLISTED NUMBERS

I'm not sure if this figure would hold up to a lot of statistical rigor, but it is often said that 75% of jobs are never listed. As in, the only way you find out about these jobs is by talking to people.

75% seems a bit high, but it makes the point. There are a TON of internships out there that don't show up on the web.

So, how do you get access to these jobs?

You talk to people. You let people know that you are looking for an internship!

When you're in internship hunting mode, go out of your way to meet new people and when you do, make sure you say explicitly, "I'm looking for an internship right now."

I can't stress this enough. So often I see students who kind of beat around the bush. They reach out and "want to have coffee."

By the way, I actually don't drink coffee. But even if I did – does having "coffee" mean that we could just sit there and drink without talking? It might get weird, but at least we'd have coffee.

No!

If you want somebody's help finding an internship, say "I'd be grateful for any help you can give me with my internship search." Or, "do you know of anyone looking for an intern? Because, I'm looking for an xyz type of internship."

Suppose you are fortunate enough to be one of the people I describe in Chapter 3; that is, you know what kind of internship you want to do. If that's you, make a list of the 4 or 5 places where you would like to intern. Then, check them out.

If you don't see information about internship program, give them a call and ask, "do you have an internship program?"

I've actually worked with organizations that purposely don't list information about their internship program online because they only want to consider applicants who are interested enough to take initiative and call.

Just because you don't see information about an internship opportunity doesn't mean it isn't there.

13 CAREER CENTERS

Believe it or not, if you're in school, there is a really good chance that your school has a career center that you can go to. Did you know that?

I must admit, when I was in college, I never visited a career center one time. What's worse, having transferred 7 times between 5 schools over the course of my college career – that means I missed FIVE different career centers.

Have you visited your school's career center? If you have, good for you! If you haven't, you should.

I never visited a career center in school because as a student, I just never thought it was relevant. Maybe if I had visited a career center, I would have had more of a clue about internships and jobs before stumbling into the working world.

If you're looking for an internship, go to your school's career center. There is a good chance that your school has an established relationship with organizations that might interest you.

Think about it, students come and go – but schools and employers tend to stay. If a student from your school was a great intern last year, that employer might really like the idea of taking another intern from your school (you) this year without needing to go through all the trouble of advertising an open internship position.

It's a little old school, but the perfect internship position for you might be hanging as a flier on the bulletin board of your college career center right now.

But, if not, your school's career center can also tell you about any structured internship program opportunities that are available. Many schools run regular "Semester in (you name the place) programs" that include excellent but often unlisted internship opportunities.

14 MAKE YOUR OWN WAY

Even though it seems like internships should be everywhere, many organizations don't have internship programs.

Why?

They don't know how.

They don't know how to put together an internship application or how to get students to apply. They don't feel confident that they can manage interns or they worry about legal ramifications of hosting an intern.

Here's the thing, running an internship program really isn't that hard. As long as an employer is acting as a mentor and a student is learning a ton – they're pretty much good to go.

There is a much debated U.S. Department of Labor regulation that states an employer shouldn't benefit from having an intern. But that's pretty vague (not to mention I think, pretty stupid).

Suffice to say, so long as an employer isn't openly exploiting student internship labor just for the sake of making extra money, and a student intern (as in, you) feel like you're learning, that's the deal.

So, if you would like to do an internship someplace, but that place doesn't offer an internship program, let them know that one of your first projects as their first intern will be to set up an internship program for them.

Don't know how to set up an internship program. Well, sounds like you're going to learn. Learning, get it? That's the whole idea.

Does approaching an employer and suggesting you act as their intern even when they don't have an internship program sound too forward to you? If it does, get over it.

Why?

Because, getting over it will give you an unfair advantage.

Let other young professionals stand down while you help a potential employer help you but helping them start an internship program.

For many employers, it's a vicious cycle. Look at it from their perspective. They're in box.

They think, "I can't afford to manage and provide a great learning experience for interns because I don't have time, and I don't have time because I'm short staffed."

You might be amazed by the number of employers that would be incredibly receptive to being approached by an eager young professional (you) who takes the initiative.

What do you have to lose?

PART III: APPLY YOURSELF

You know what kind of internship you want and why you want it. Just as importantly, you've found it.

But this is where the rubber meets the road. Now we turn to the internship application process and what you need to do in order to make your application great.

If you're lucky, you've managed to get an internship without having to apply formally. But in the majority of situations, at some point you'll find yourself looking at a blank application form.

Now what?

15 YOU WANT A RELATIONSHIP?

First, back up a bit.

Before you even get to the point where you have an application in your hand, there are some things to do.

What if your first contact with a possible internship host had nothing to do with your asking for an internship? What if, instead, it revolved around your showing results in advance?

"Results in advance…what's that?!"

Results in advance means you do a little homework to find out what an employer is interested in, or what they need help with. This is way easier than it sounds.

Let's say you decide that you want to be the world's expert on synthetic worm fish lures and, because they are some of the best in the world when it comes to fake worms, you want to intern with Bob's Tackle Shop.

First, find out what Bob needs. Go to his website, what sorts of things are Bob and the other folks at the shop talking about? What problems do they have?

Is there anything that they are missing?

"But! What if Bob doesn't even have a website?"Well then your work is

easy – help Bob establish a website!

Radical thought: reach out to Bob and let him know you are interested in starting a career that revolves around fake worms. Ask him if he wouldn't mind meeting with you.

People are flattered when you seek their advice. 99% of the time the Bobs of the world are going to welcome meeting with anybody to talk about their business and their career.

When you meet with Bob, ask him what might make his business better. Ask him what he's tried that hasn't worked. When you leave, say "thank you very much."

Then you follow up. Take some steps that might help Bob solve some of his problems. Suppose Bob said one of his issues has to do with displaying all the fake worms to customers. What would happen if you wrote up a plan or diagram about how the fake worms might be displayed in a better way and then you sent that plan to Bob with a nice note? What if you did some research about how other stores display their fake worms and wrote up a summary for Bob? Do you think Bob would like this. You bet he would.

Do this a couple of times. Stay in touch with Bob…ask for nothing in return.

When the time comes to approach him about doing an internship, do you think Bob will be receptive? Absolutely.

Why, because you've already showed Bob that 1) you care about his business and 2) you are capable of adding value to his business.

The best foundation for anyone applying to be an intern is to show results in advance.

Give first and you shall receive.

Disclaimer: your warming up to a potential internship employer can't be B.S., it's got to be genuine. In other words, if you really don't care about a potential employer or their work and you're just trying to get close to put an internship on your resume, it won't work. They'll know.

On the other hand, if you are genuinely interested in what a potential employer is doing, then offering them results in advance of your internship will be easy.

Second disclaimer: does this sound like a lot of extra work? It is.

Are you unwilling to take this extra step? That's ok, just don't be surprised if/when you don't get the internship.

Will "results in advance" always work? No. But it will help your chances a ton if you're willing to do it.

Third disclaimer: what if you just can't figure out how to make contact with the "Bob" where you want to do an internship? With a little work, it's pretty rare that you can't find somebody's telephone and email address. At the very least you can find their mailing address. Here are some tricks:

When it comes to email addresses sometimes a simple google search will do it. If that doesn't work, try googling their name with their organization's @domain name. For example, you could search for "Bob Smith" + "@btackleshp.com"

Often, companies will use the same naming conventions for email addresses.

So, if you see that Suzie Jones at the tackle shop is SJones@btackleshp.com, then BSmith@btackleshp.com is worth a try for Bob.

This is a situation where something like LinkedIn can be helpful. Look to see if you know somebody who knows Bob and might be willing to introduce you.

Ask around to family, friends, and relatives to see if anybody is in a position to introduce you.

Lastly a simple phone call to Bob's office might do the trick. Even if you're only able to reach Bob's assistant, chances are that he or she will be willing to convey your message.

16 BUILD YOUR CAMPAIGN

Ok…so you've built a relationship with a potential internship host that is based on your offering them genuine results in advance. Time to send in that application, right?

Easy Trigger, not yet.

You should treat the application process to an internship like a campaign. In order to wage a campaign, you need great campaign materials. How are yours?

What sort of campaign materials do you need? Here is a good list:

Resume

Letter

Testimonial/Reference sheet

Creative Resume/One Sheets

Social Media Footprint

Online Portfolio

Do you need ALL of this stuff to get an internship? No. But the more you have, the greater the chance you get the internship you want.

Let's take each of these pieces in turn…

Resume

Several volumes could be devoted to the subject of resumes. But, without getting too far into the weeds – let me give you some crash suggestions…

Approach some people you respect and ask if you can see an example of their resume and whether they would be willing to take a look at yours to offer suggestions. If you approach even just two or three people like this, your resume will be better.

Make sure your resume tells your story. You may say, "but! I don'thave a lot of work experience to put on a resume!" That's fine, but I still bet you have a story – use your resume to tell your story.

Skip dorky things like "Objectives" or "References Available Upon Request." You don't need them.

Make your resume one page. Yes, one page. Think you can't fit all your stuff on one page? See all that white space around the outside of your resume? Fill it in.

If you're just starting out and aren't sure where to start with a resume, do this. Put your name and contact information at the top. Then, create three sections going down the page in this order: Education, Experience, Other. Then fill each of those sections to the hilt.

Unless you're applying to do an internship at a graphic design company, your resume doesn't have to look pretty, it just needs to be readable.

In the end, a reviewer might only spend about ten seconds looking at your resume. The purpose of the resume is to give them a reason to put yours in the good pile and not the bad pile.

Make sure your resume is explicit in the way it says "here is why you should put me in the good pile." Let your resume reach out and bash the reviewer over the head with that message.

Letter

Yes, whenever you send a resume to somebody, you also need to send a letter. Every time.

"But! They don't ask for a letter!" I don't care. Send a letter. If you're lucky, nobody else applying to the internship will send a letter and the fact that you did alone will make you stand out.

So, what should the letter say?

The formula is pretty simple…here it is:

"Dear Bob (or if need be Dear Bob's Tackle Shop),

If you hire me as an intern, I could do a lot to help you and your organization."

(Then you write about all the awesome stuff you could do for them)

If you think I might be a good fit, I would love to have the opportunity to contribute to you and your colleagues' important work to (fill in what they do). Or, if not, best wishes for finding a great candidate. Either way, thank you in advance for your consideration.

Sincerely, (You)"

That's it.

Of course, feel free to adjust the words and/or put this in your own voice.

What I want you to understand is that your letter should 1) mostly be about what you can do for a potential internship host and 2) come from a place of confidence, not desperation.

Too often I see cover letters that focus mainly on what the internship will do for the applicant. Phrases like, "your internship would really help me meet my career goals" should have NO place in your letter. Savvy?

Testimonial/Reference Sheet

A great testimonial/reference sheet is another vital secret weapon you can employ during your internship search to give yourself an unfair advantage.

What the heck is a testimonial/reference sheet? It's easy. Whenever somebody says something nice about you, write it down (or ideally, ask them to repeat it while you video tape them)! Then, just write down those quotes on a piece of paper.

If you haven't been collecting quotes like that, start now. In the meantime, for immediate purposes, approach some of your teachers, friends, past employers and ask them to send you a quick quote. Put them all down on a piece of paper and you'll be amazed how great it makes you look.

On the same piece of paper, put down the names and contact information (name, title, organization, telephone, email) for 3-5 people who have agreed to serve as a reference for you. Can some of the people you list as a reference be the same people you quote? Of course.

Note about letters of reference: some internship programs will ask you for a certain number of letters of reference. If you don't have a good file of such letters already built up, start now. Instead of asking for a simple quote, ask some of your allies for a full letter. Then quote from it or use the full letter as you need to. **When you can, always get letters of references written generically to "Whom it May Concern" and get a copy for yourself.** That way, you can use them over and over and over as you need to.

Creative Resumes and One-Sheet

Do me a favor, sit down in front of a computer and Google the term "creative resumes."

See what I mean? Do you suddenly feel boring?

If you're not in front of a computer and are wondering what the heck I'm talking about…creative resumes are essentially resumes that don't look like a resume at all. Quilt a resume, do it as a poem, make it look like eBay…those are creative resumes.

If you were going through a stack of resumes and ran into a hand painted resume, do you think it would get your attention? You bet it would. Would you be impressed/what to talk to that candidate?

It depends. But studies are increasingly showing that creative resumes work. I know that when I encounter something creative, I almost always want to at least talk to that person. **People greatly underestimate the level of boredom in the working world and how much employers are interested in finding something new.**

Why do creative resumes work? They're risky, which makes them rare. Because they're rare, they seem valuable. When your resume seems valuable, so do you.

Will creative resumes work in every situation? Probably not. If you're applying for an internship with "Stuffy Gray Suit Banker Inc."…maybe you hold the creative version back. Or, if you're doing battle with some kind of online application form that won't take a creative resume – you don't really have too much of a choice (unless you want to really take initiative and get that creative resume to the employer by somehow bypassing the system… hint, hint.).

So, maybe you maintain two versions of your resume….the more traditional one and the creative one. By all means, let the knowledge that creative resumes are out there free your thinking about whether your resume looks "formal" enough.

Another option is to include a one-sheet with a traditional resume.

Hollywood has a long tradition of pitching movie ideas to producers and ultimately move-goers through "one-sheets." You should use a one-sheet to pitch yourself to a potential internship employer.

What is a one-sheet? In the movie business it's basically one sheet of paper that summarizes a product for publicity and sales. The movies ones are often great big; you can do yours on a regular sheet of paper.

Be creative, use pictures, create a small poster that is going to grab the attention of the reviewer and suggest all the amazing things you can do for their organization if they choose you as an intern.

You might ask, "But! Doesn't my resume give all the relevant information I need to give out about myself?"

You're right, it does. But different people absorb different information in different ways and your internship campaign is all about making yourself stand out.

Social Media Footprint

Some young professionals are still a little skittish about social media because they're worried about privacy or potential employers seeing their latest drunken adventures.

Get over it.

These days, not having a social media presence is almost more suspicious than any drunken photos that might wind up online.

Not everybody agrees with me on this point, but I believe that having a social media presence will soon be more important than letters, resumes…all of it.

If you're behind on your social media skills and/or establishing an online presence, then start now.

"But , What if a potential employer sees my crazy photos from Spring Break?!?"

My answer is: what if they do? If they are diving into your personal stuff and they are going to be thrown off by your personal stuff – then you don't want to do an internship with them anyway.

On the other hand if you put yourself out there on all channels as an authentic human being, I believe it will make you stand out as a real and interesting person. I believe it will make you stand out as someone who is fearless, has passion, who isn't afraid to get their hands dirty, the sort of person that most good managers would want to hire as an intern.

After all, if you hide who you are either through social media omission or concealment, isn't that a lie? Most employers I know don't like to hire liars.

Online Portfolio

Building an online portfolio is similar to establishing a social media presence, but by "Online Portfolio" I mean something more specific.

Start a space; it can be a fancy webpage like yourname.com, but it doesn't have to be. There are a ton of online tools that can help you do this (about.me, blogger, tumblr, etc.) Build a place online where you can display your best work: writing, photos, movies, art – all of it.

By creating this reservoir of your genius, it gives you a place of reference that can be used for all your internship campaign materials. Instead of mentioning something you did, hyperlink that mention to a movie that shows it. Rather than simply describe a project you led, hyperlink to pictures that show it.

Very powerful don't you think? I do. I think it's powerful enough to give you a real unfair advantage during your internship quest.

Once you build up an arsenal of materials to wage your internship campaign (I hope you do), you are in much better position to start applying for internships.

Here's a bonus: once you have this arsenal and get into the habit of maintaining it – keeping your resume current, adding items to your online portfolio, etc – you'll never have to recreate it from scratch again.

Where other candidates for internships and jobs may get caught flat footed, your stuff will be ready to go.

17 APPLICATION MATTERS

Congratulations! Now that you have a deep reservoir of highly effective internship campaign materials, you are a heavy hitter. You need not worry about the amazing competition that could blindside you in the race to find a great internship, because that amazing competition is now YOU!

But even with your war chest of amazing application materials, there are still a few things to think about when you are actually at the point where you send off an internship application.

Aside from filling out forms that ask for your name, address, etc., it is not uncommon for potential internship hosts to ask you for an essay or two.

The subjects you as an applicant may be asked to write about can vary widely. In writing essays for an internship application, keep two things in mind:

First, be authentic. Be crazy authentic. Don't sand down any of your edges because you think that's what the reader will want to see. Let everybody else do that while you maintain extreme authenticity. If you do, you'll stand out and that's exactly what you want to do (more on this to come).

Second, maintain your cover letter theme of: this is what I can do for you. A lot of the essays coming from your competitors may focus on "this internship will be good for me as a student because..." Contrast yourself against other applicants by making sure a running theme through all your essays is **"this is what I can do for you. "**

Be the authentic applicant focused on what you can contribute through the internship. Let that come out in every component of your application.

18 DIVERSIFY YOUR PORTFOLIO

Some people believe that internships exclude.

That is, the only way most students can get an internship is if their dad knows some muckity-muck or their mom is friends with somebody at the country club. They cast internships as a really blue-blooded affair.

I think a lot of critics get this wrong.

I've seen many more examples where employers have used internships to diversify their workforce and seek out candidates that, where there no internships, they might not otherwise encounter.

Even though it's usually illegal, is it conceivable that you will be discriminated against because of your unusual or humble background? I won't sugar coat it (and if this applies to you, you probably don't need me to) – it's absolutely possible.

But here is the thing, if a potential internship employer is going to discriminate against you because you're gay, or because of your ethnicity, or your religion, do you think that employer is going to be much of a mentor?

$%^# `em.

On the other hand, let's say you don't try to conceal who you are. You put down that you worked as a missionary for two years, you put down that you competed in the beauty pageant, you fess up to being a member of the anarchist sensitivity drum circle.

Well, I don't know about you, but I'd at least want to MEET somebody who has that drum circle down on their resume.

My point is, don't try and cover up who you are. I believe it's more likely that potential employers (and especially any that are worth working for) will be more likely to hire you because you're different than not.

19 OPEN THE KIMONO

Author Tim Ferriss talks about "opening the kimono;" I'd like to take this opportunity to steal that line.

What do I mean by "opening the kimono" in terms of your social media profile? Well it means that you should listen to all those people who are telling you to take all the questionable photos off of Facebook and that you shouldn't say anything blatantly political on Twitter.

You should listen to them and then completely ignore them.

If a potential employer is going to search around for you online and choose to enter your personal world, then they do so at their own risk. If they are any sort of worthwhile human being, they will understand that everybody is human and the fact that you are too only means you're going to be a better intern.

Everybody puts their shorts on one leg at a time.

So I say: don't clean up a thing. Be authentic, let all your competitors in the application process sanitize their social media stuff so you can stand out.

Let me ask you this. In cleaning up your social media footprint so you look good for potential employers...isn't that kind of lying?

The hard part about lying is, once you do it, maintaining the lie becomes exhausting. If you conceal something about who you are to a potential employer, how soon will it be before they discover the truth and when they do, what will happen?

If you had fun on spring break, leave those photos up there.

20 RESEARCH BLEESEARCH

If you love research, good for you!

I have a love-hate relationship with research. If I'm looking into something I don't care about, research is like nails on a chalk board for me (that's bad, by the way).

On the other hand, if I'm trying to figure out what makes a person or organization tick, I'll spend hours getting all the intel I can about them. This is when I wonder if I would have been an excellent spy. But, I digress. Or, do I?

The point here is straightforward, if you're going to make the material in your internship application war chest the best it can be, then you're going to need to do a little research.

You don't need to spend a ton of time doing it, even 10 minutes of focused time might be enough. You want to look for things that an organization has chosen to highlight prominently. Chances are, those are the things that are central to their mission and, to the people involved with deciding to hire you as an intern, really important.

When you see issues displayed prominently by an organizations, those are your "omens." Those are the things to focus on. How can you help an organization do better when it comes to those omens?

21 BREAK RULES

When your application instructions suggest you should only submit two essays, why not submit three?

Do you run the risk that the evaluator of your application will ding you for not following rules to the letter? It's possible. But, I think it's more likely that by not following the rules to the letter, you'll just stand out as being extra awesome.

For example, if an application requires you to send a resume, send a cover letter too. If the application asks for information from you, why not send it as a poem, or a video, or a collage.

Is this approach a little risky? Yes. But, that's why it's probably worth doing.

Of course, you've got to walk a fine line here. You don't want to get so far outside the parameters of what your potential internship employer is looking for that you get too far afield.

But, if you can walk that line and break the rules just a little bit, you'll benefit in at least two ways.

First, breaking the rules will allow you to send more. You can send more examples of your work that demonstrate that you are awesome. Use as much of that internship application campaign war chest of materials as you can.

Second, by sending stuff that others don't, you stand out. I may have a stack of resumes with cover letters stapled in front. But, if I catch a glimpse of something neon yellow in the pile (the thing you were brave enough to send) – chances are I'm going to pull that one from the pile first just to see what the hell it is.

Break the rules and be different. Just because internship application instructions don't explicitly say you can do something doesn't mean you can't.

22 TIMING IS EVERYTHING

Let me paint a picture for you about the life of a typical internship hiring manager.

After putting out a call for internships applicants, an internship coordinator is accustomed to hearing NOTHING for the longest time.

Then, maybe a day or two before the application deadline, there is this tsunami of internship applications. At the same time, the coordinator can expect to start getting a ton of calls from applicants with questions about the application.

In addition, there will likely be more than one applicant that calls to find out if there is any way they can send their application in after the deadline because of a variety of excuses.

What if an internship hiring manager received your application a day or two after they sent out a call for applicants?

What if between the time you sent in your application and the deadline, you sent the internship coordinator or host organization something that might help them (remember Chapter 15)?

Do you think your early application, along with your willingness to show results in advance, would make the internship coordinator think that you were highly organized and helpful? I think it would.

Here's another angle: if that internship coordinator is just looking for a reason to choose one application over another – is the fact that your application was the first she received give her a reason to choose your application over another? It totally does.

When your internship application is the first one an organization receives, way ahead of all the rest, it's going to get noticed and either consciously or unconsciously the person evaluating that application is going to give you a bump for being first.

23 AN INTERN FOR EVERY SEASON

When you're gunning for an internship, be aware that the supply of interns in the universe often varies.

Typically, your competition for a summer internship is going to be way more intense than fall or spring. **So if you're applying for a dream internship, and you have the option – definitely stay away from summer.**

Along those same lines – organizations are often strapped for help between the traditional times student interns are available – usually August and May. So if you let a potential internship host know that you are willing and able to serve when most other students can't or won't, your chances of getting into that internship you want are much, much greater.

Bear in mind that employers often looki for interns who can best fulfill their needs at times when they can offer the greatest learning experiences. This means that the greater flexibility you can offer in terms of your availability, the more attractive an applicant you will be.

When putting together an internship application, put down as much flexibility on your schedule as you can honestly and conceivably imagine. Realize when you do that you're not making any commitments about your time yet by simply listing your availability. Rather, you're just indicating times you might be available to work if you are accepted.

When you are accepted to the internship, you can work out your work schedule then. Understand that on the application, you want to remain honest, but you also don't want to pass up any opportunity to make yourself appear as the best candidate possible.

PART IV: LAND THAT INTERNSHIP

You know what kind of internship you want, where it is, and you've applied to it – now it's time to stick the landing and make it your own.

If you've taken the extra time and effort so far, there is a good chance that you will stand out like a sore thumb among applicants for the internship you seek.

Is it always a sure thing? Of course not. There might be factors standing between you and the internship you seek that are outside your control. But if you've approached the internship quest in the right way – hopefully the organization hosting that internship has been properly wowed.

What do you do now?!?

24 E.T. PHONE HOME

If your application has found its way into the right pile, you might get a letter straight away saying the internship is yours. Increasing however – maybe because of competitive inflation – intern hosts are reaching out to potential candidates for interview.

It might be a phone interview, it might be an interview in person, it might be a combination of both. Whichever way things go down, you want to be prepared. Let us start with the phone interview; some of what I described here will apply equally well to in-person interviews, which we'll talk about next.

When you apply for an internship and a potential internship host reaches back out to arrange a phone interview, you've got to decide how much of a priority that particular internship opportunity is for you.

This may sound a little hard core, but I think it's a pretty black and white sort of thing. That is, either you don't care at all about this internship or it's a really big deal for you.

If you don't care, politely let the host know that you appreciate their reaching out, but you're not interested.

On the other hand, if getting this internship is a big deal for you, then you should treat it as such.

What does this mean? It means when they ask when you might be available to do a phone interview, your answer back to them is "at your convenience." That's right – if you need to, you skip class, skip work – you **do whatever you need to do to convey that this internship is a priority for you and you're willing to move mountains to make the potential internship host's life easier.**

Now, I suppose there might be a few exceptions – sick loved one, major exam that can't be rescheduled, etc. But, for the most part, you frame the phone interview so it's at the interviewer's convenience.

Next, you do the interview on the best sounding line in the quietest place you can. This is a bigger deal than you might suppose. Cell phones and Skype are so ubiquitous nowadays that you might think they are ok for an interview, but they're not. You want to sound crystal clear to an interviewer. Do anything you can to do that interview call from a hard line. If the interviewer is planning to call you, this might take some planning on your part to figure out where you'll be, and when.

If you've ever watched any of the political pundit spin shows (these are some of my favorite shows to watch) you may notice that the talking heads tend to be really good at delivering certain talking points, regardless of what question is asked. Within reason, this should be your strategy during an interview.

Before you sit down for that phone interview, think of 3 or 4 messages that you want to deliver to your interviewer. The messages can be simple, like "I'm a great manager" or "I'm very detail oriented." Come up with some scripts and stories that will permit you to deliver those talking points in response to a variety of questions.

The fun part about a phone interview is that it's a lot like an open book test in the sense that you can have all your notes ready to go, laid out in front of you, before the interview even starts.

For an in-person interview, things must come a bit more from memory.

25 NICE TO MEET YOU

For an in-person interview, your tactics are a little bit different.

I could probably write an entire book on interview tactics alone (maybe I will!). But for now, here is your crash course.

Get to your interview spot about 30 minutes ahead of time…but walk on by, don't go in. Find a place nearby to look over your notes one last time, get a drink, cool off…check your look – whatever you want to do. Then, time it so you walk into the interview spot about 5 minutes before you're start time. Never, ever, ever be late for an interview.

Wear a suit. Unless you're interviewing to intern at a fashion outlet or some offbeat place, don't worry about getting creative. Your goal is to look, professional. You may be overdressed, that's ok.

Carry pen and paper, you're going to be taking notes during the interview.

Turn all your electronics off. No cell phones going off during the interview.

Carry several copies of your resume with you so if your interviewer asks, "do you have a copy of your resume with you?" you will.

If when you arrive the interviewer seems rushed or suggests you speak while she goes to get lunch, if you get the sense the that the interviewer isn't showing you very much respect…just very politely ask if there would be a better time for you to come back to do the interview. Some interviewers will use this technique to rattle you – they make you do the interview in the lunch line etc. Don't fall for it. If you push back just a bit, you'll beat the interviewer at this game.

Once you're face to face with your interviewer, do what I described for the phone interview. Use your message talking points to respond to the questions, even if they don't completely answer the questions the interviewer is asking.

Don't be afraid to let the interviewer do a lot of talking, but if the conversation gets too far off, don't be afraid to politely steer it back to why you would be the best intern this organization could ever hope to have.

Be prepared with a question or two for the interviewer – because they will probably ask you if you have any questions. When they do, you should. Make sure you ask about something that you couldn't just as easily look up on your own.

Most important: remember that the interviewer puts on their shorts one leg at a time just like everybody else. There is no reason for you to be intimidated or lack confidence.

26 THANK YOU

I used to think that sending hand written notes following an interview was the best way to go because an applicant really stand out. But nowadays, that's just too slow.

Either later in the day or the next day following an interview, send a thank you note to your interviewer and anybody else you might conceivably need to thank. It doesn't have to be long, it doesn't even really need to reiterate why you would be the best person for their internship position. More than anything, it just needs to be genuine.

Let the interviewer know that you are grateful for the opportunity to meet them and if there was anything you found particularly interesting or enjoyable about the interview, let them know. Offer to provide any more info that would be helpful. But that's pretty much it.

Be a grateful young professional, don't be a stalker.

27 CAN I GET A WITNESS?

This may be something you already lined up when you first applied for the internships. But, if not, it's something you need to do before an interview or very soon after an interview: line up your references.

Get into the habit of keeping a current list of supervisors, peers, and if you have them, subordinates who can speak about how awesome you are.

Sometime around the interview stage, potential internship employers may ask you for the names and contact info of people you've worked with who can vouch for you as a good human being. Have this list ready.

Beyond just names and contact info – put a little blub next to each about how you know each person.

Give each of these people a heads up whenever you think it's possible a potential internship employer might reach out to them. Not only is this a polite thing to do for your references, but it will very likely equip them to say just the right thing about you, depending on the opportunity at hand.

Don't be afraid to use your references proactively. If this is an internship you really want (it is right? this is all or nothing right?) – if you have any references that would be in a particularly good position to do so, ask them to reach out to the potential employer proactively and sing your praises.

As a potential internship host, if I get several emails and calls voicing the particular merits of a particular candidate, I'm going to look at that candidate for sure.

Is this a little heavy handed? Yes. Is it a little aggressive? You bet. Will it give you an unfair advantage. Absolutely.

28 YOU HAVE NOTHING TO LOSE

So you've gone all in. You've found the right internship, you've sent in awesome materials with your application, you did everything just right with the interview, and now…nothing. You haven't heard squat.

Take satisfaction in knowing that you're in good company. This is a story that is incredibly common. What does it mean when you don't hear back?

Is it possible that they've hired somebody else? Is it possible that they've decided not hire anybody? Is it possible that a key decision maker is out sick? Is it possible that you offended them horribly? Is it possible they sent you an email and it just didn't go through?

Yep.

If the time period when a potential internship host committed to get back to you has come and gone, there's only one thing you can do: follow-up with them.

Now, don't get me wrong…I'm not talking about a situation where you interviewed on Monday and you're just anxious so you reach out to them on Wednesday.

Rather, if it's a been a couple of weeks and/or several days past the time they promised they would get back to you – reach out to them. You have nothing to lose.

When one has gone through all the hurdles with a possible internship and then hears nothing, the most likely cause is one of two things.

Either the potential employer has picked somebody else and they haven't been competent or decent enough to let you know. Or they've just gotten busy and haven't had a chance to move forward on recruiting you as an intern.

When you follow-up in the former case, you find out and can move on. When you follow-up in the later, you might give the employer just the reminder they need to move the ball forward on getting you into the office.

It may feel safe to just wait on hearing back, but it's not. Don't be an ostrich with you head in the sand. Follow up. Either they want you or they don't. If they don't, somebody else will be lucky to get you.

Your time, especially the early years of your career are very valuable.

Don't permit anybody to waste your time.

29 DON'T MAKE THEM SORRY THEY CHOSE YOU

Something terrific happens. You get the call/email/letter from the employer of your dreams saying, "YES! We want you to come be our intern!"

Good for you! Now you can relax, kick back, and let it all hang out right? No way.

I've seen plenty of examples where internship applicants undergo a radical transformation when they get accepted into an internship program. Before getting accepted, they seem awesome but after getting accepted, they turn into dorks.

Don't be a dork when you land the internship of your dreams.

If you do start acting like a dork, is there anything to prevent an employer from retracting their internship offer? In most cases, there isn't. Internships aren't like getting into college in the sense that once you're in, you're in.

In fact, in the vast majority of internships an employer can get rid of you with very little cause. FYI - this is true in a lot of jobs too. Welcome to the working world and congratulations on encountering another lesson internships can provide: job interviews really never quit.

It is sometimes said that an internship is just an extended job interview. I believe this is very true.

What does this mean for you? It means that once you land that dream internship, pat yourself on the back for about 5 minutes. Then move forward on the premise that you're going to have to work every day to keep it.

PART V: ROADBLOCKS

You've constructed an incredibly impressive campaign to land that perfect internship, it seems like a sure-thing. What happens if you still don't get it? What happens if they call you and say "no?" What happens if you get the rejection letter?

Well, one of the first lessons applying for an internship can teach is that, in the real working world, very rarely is anything a "sure-thing."

So what should you do if you hit the end of the road with your internship quest? Answer: turn around, get back on the road and find another way.

Here's how.

30 EXTRA CREDIT

They said "no."

They said you were really impressive but they just aren't able to take you because they received applications from so many well qualified applicants.

Here's a secret for you that may make you feel better, or it may make you feel worse: employers can almost always take one more. There's always a way. The cutoff is usually more based on their capacity to host interns: desks, computers, an amount of work, could be anything.

The bad news here, without sugar coating it at all is, for whatever reason…you got outcompeted. You lost. For sanity's sake, assume it was more to do with circumstances than it had to do with you. But still, you lost.

However! The good news is that when they say, "they can't take you as an intern." They actually are lying. What they're really saying is, "due to limits of our operation, we choose not to accept you as an intern." If they really really really wanted to take you, could they? Yes.

So if this is an internship you really want, give it one more shot. Send them a writing sample or a video explaining why it would really be in their interest to reconsider.

Now, don't go stalker. This is a very subtle business. You want to convey that you are tenacious and reluctant to give up – those are good traits. You don't want to convey that you are obsessive and don't listen – those are bad traits.

If you are the only applicant who follows-up like this and all the other rejectees don't – the organization may just decide they have room for one more.

This is a one shot deal, if the response to your final overture is another polite rejection or even radio silence, let it go. You're not in the business of burning bridges.

However, if this internship is the one you really want – make this last ditch try. You might be surprised.

31 HONEST FEEDBACK

This is one of the savviest things you can do when you receive a rejection, and it's something that so many applicants never do, ask for feedback.

A lot of times people sending a rejection message will include something about wishing you the best of luck or an offer to be helpful in your career. Take them up their offer, immediately.

How? **Ask the person who just rejected you how your application could have been better.** This will instantly accomplish an incredible variety of things.

First, it shows the employer who just rejected you that you are incredibly mature and that you're not the sort of person who takes rejection personally. Being such an un-sore looser makes you look good.

Second, believe it or not, that person who just rejected you feels bad. They WANT to make it up to you somehow. By asking for feedback you give that employer who just rejected you a chance to make it up to you. In my experience, they will really spend time to give you valuable feedback.

Third: this employer just rejected you – the relationship you have with them is now an open bleeding wound. It can't get any worse. So, the employer has no reason not to give you completely honest unvarnished feedback. They have not need to be polite, they've basically already told you that you suck compared to others. As a young professional, this sort of unvarnished honest feedback is often the hardest to get as a young professional because most well-meaning mentors care about you too much to risk hurting your feelings. But not these bastards, they just rejected you. Take advantage of it!

32 I'LL BE BACK!

During my spring semester of freshman year of college I failed chemistry. It was the first F I ever received.

So that summer, I retook chemistry and got an A. That A was all the more satisfying because I failed the first time.

If you fall short on the first attempt to land an internship, and decide you want to try again, tell the employer you'll be back.

Again, you want to do this in a way that conveys you are tenacious, not a stalker. Just let the employer know that you care so much about this opportunity that you are going to try again. Then repeat your campaign a second time, incorporating what you learned the first time.

When that employer sees your stuff come in, they may dismiss you. But chances are greater they will admire your attitude and as a result, stick you at the top of the list.

Is it a sure-fire thing? No. But there's no better way to express that you're truly passionate about an opportunity than by getting back on the horse after you've been shot down. Try it.

33 NO SKILLS, NO EXPERIENCE

If you've gotten through all this material and you're thinking, "well this is all fine and good, but I won't be able to do any of this until I actually have a resume"…we'll I'm sorry to say you've got the wrong idea.

You have a resume, whether you know it or not, you have one.

You may not have ever been paid for work you've done, but I guarantee you've done work, you have achievements, you have skills. That's your resume.

Don't feel like you have to have a bunch of really official sounding titles, or that you need to have received a regular paycheck for something to count as a "job." In fact, more and more, the sort of experience employers are looking for actually doesn't meet that definition.

Now, it may be that you have experience and skills but you want better experience and better skills. Well, if that's the case, go get them. Getting the right internship might just help you do that.

Just remember, everybody in the world who has more skills and experience than you do – at one time – at some point was exactly where you are now. They just learned more; so can you.